I0202961

Faith Favor Grace

Gyfted Ink LLC

Books may be purchased by contacting the publisher and author at:

gyftedink@gmail.com

Publisher: Gyfted Ink, a division of Gyfted Ink, LLC

Editor: Melissa Henry Stover

Creative Consultant: To God be the glory

Library of Congress Catalog Number: 2015906524

{Gyfted Ink LLC} {Lugoff, SC}

ISBN-13: 978-0692432242

ISBN-10: 0692432248

1. Spirituality 2. Self Help

First Edition

Printed in United States

FAITH FAVOR GRACE

POETRY FOR THE SOUL

BY

MELISSA HENRY STOVER

YOUR SOUL

You may be blessed with silver and gold

Nothing compares to the value of your soul

God gave his only son so that you may live

So being obedient is a small price to give

Jesus Christ shed his blood on Calvary

He gave his life so that we may be free

Free from bondage, burden, and sin

You don't have to fight you are destined to win

So give God the glory and let him lead the way

He gave his son so that you may be blessed everyday

YOU MUST

You must go through something to be something

You must cry before you laugh

You must have pain before you have joy

You must mourn before you rejoice

You must crawl before you can walk

You must die to be reborn

YOU

My life was nothing until you came in

You filled me with joy and freed me from sin

You washed me clean, and made me white as snow

You nurtured me, encouraged me, and watched me grow

You took my hand, and gently led the way

You promised that you would not lead me astray

You are my Savior, and I'll worship you all my days

In my mouth shall continually be your praise

HE PROMISED

He promised me he would love me and never walk away

He promised to lead me in the right direction and never astray

He promised to protect me and never leave me alone

He promised to watch over me and bless my home

He promised to hold me tight when nights are cold

He promised to take care of me even when I grow old

He promised to be my husband, and me his faithful wife

He promised if I obeyed him that I shall have eternal life

THEY

They hung him on the cross, and left him there to die

Jesus gave his precious life for sinners like you and I

They laughed, they mocked him, and they hung him in shame

He said, Father forgive them, not one did he blame

They put thorns on his head, and pierced his side

He forgave them all with arms open wide

They stood there and watched as he slipped away

Not knowing what a price that he had just paid

BLESSING YOU

Just because he left, you feel you can't go on

Dry your eyes my sister, because joy comes in the morn

Just because he left you don't see any reason to live

Give your old life to Jesus, and a new life he will give

Just because he left, you feel you weren't a good wife

Did you ever stop to think, that God took the bad out of your life

Just because he left, you feel hurt, betrayed, and ashamed

Girl after all he did to you, why should you carry the blame

The next time you think of him, and you feel a little blue

Open your eyes and realize, that God was just blessing you

DRY YOU'RE EYES

Dry your eyes my sister, help is on the way

God will send you angels each and everyday

Dry your eyes my sister, your struggle is at the end

God says that your blessings are just about to begin

Dry your eyes my sister, blessings are on the other side of through

God says if you just believe in him, there is nothing that he can't do

BLESS MY CHILDREN

Lord blesses my children, bless them everyday

Lord please bless me to show them the way

Lord keeps my babies from any hurt and harm

Lord teach me to forgive them with open arms

Lord bless my children in everything they do

Lord when they look at me, I pray they see you

BLESS US

Father bless us today as we become one

We pray that in this marriage, your will be done

Help us to love each other, as you love us all

Help us to catch each other if one should ever fall

Help us to have a marriage that would reflect you

And may people see you in everything we do

GOD SAID

You said I would die: God said I would live

You said I'll take it all: God began to give

You said I'll take your health: God made me well

You said I'll take your husband: God said no demon in hell

You said I'll take your house: God gave me shelter from the storm

You said Ill destroy you: God said no weapon shall form

You said Ill block your path: God gave me the will

You said I'll send a storm: God said peace be still

TURN IT OVER

Everything seems hopeless, and you don't have the strength to press on.

Fall on your knees and pray to your Father, he will make you strong.

The day seems dark and the clouds are hanging low.

Look forward to tomorrow, because if he said it, then it is so.

You feel as if you are standing all alone in the rain.

Let God carry your burden, for only he can ease your pain.

When you feel that your burden is too heavy and you want to turn back

Turn your troubles over to Christ Jesus, I promise he will take up the slack

POOR MANS ANTHEM

When the baby is crying, the phone is ringing, and all the bills are due

Don't worry, don't fret say Lord I'm giving it up to you

When the bill collector is at the door, and you don't know what to say

Turn it over to Christ Jesus, he will make a way

When you are weak and weary and your bills you can't afford to send

Ask your savior for a helping hand, and a hand he will surely lend

When your car note is late, your light bill is due and your gas hand is way past E

Remember our father in heaven has many mansions filled with blessings for you and me

When you feel your life is so bad, a future you cannot see

Take a look at the hungry and the homeless, and say Lord I thank you for blessing me

MY LIFE

As I look over my life, I'd have to say

My Lord and Savior has brought me a long way

The times I look back, I should have been gone

But God held my hand and encouraged me to carry on

I felt I should just give up and live in sin

But God said keep going I'm counting on you to win

So I struggled and I fought and never gave up faith

Knowing my prize would be to one day enter the pearly gates

NEVER GIVE UP

When you're feeling weary, and you can't go on

Our Father in Heaven will always make you strong

When you feel you're at the end of your line

Remember he may not come when you want him, but he's always on time

When you feel your struggle is at the very end

Call on Jesus an angel he will send

When you need a blessing before the setting of the sun

Cry out to our Father and he will reply it is done

Never let Satan stand in your way

Because with our Father you can begin anew each day

MY LIFE

My life was perfect until that very day

In an instant my life was forever changed

I cried myself to sleep and cried my last tear

Then I vowed I would never live my life in fear

I will never let them see me give up hope

I know it will be hard but God will help me cope

I am a fighter and I know I will survive

God has purpose for me that am why he saved my life

IF

If I could have just said goodbye

If I could have said please don't cry

If I could have said I love you

If I could have said I'll miss you too

If I could have said please forgive me

If I could have said marry me

If I could have said is it a girl or a boy

If I could have said you fill my heart with joy

If I could have said I love you mom and dad

If I could have said you're the best child a dad could have

If I could have said one more thing to you

It would have been I love you

MISSING YOU

NOT A DAY GOES BY THAT I DON'T FEEL THE PAIN

OF KNOWING I WILL NEVER SEE YOU AGAIN

NOT AN HOUR OR A MINUTE THAT YOU ARE NOT ON MY MIND

THAT SMILE AND THAT GIGGLE NEVER AGAIN WILL I FIND

THE DAY YOU LEFT A PIECE OF ME WENT WITH YOU

MY HEART IS SO HEAVY AND I DON'T KNOW WHAT TO DO

THIS PAIN THAT I FEEL CAN NEVER BE ERASED

BECAUSE A PIECE OF MY SOUL CAN NEVER BE REPLACED

Have You

Have you been a blessing to someone today?

Tell me for anyone did you go out of your way

Did you do something that you didn't want to do?

Did you stop to think they might be hungrier than you?

Did you stop and think maybe I can make her smile

Or maybe they'll feel better if I just visit them for a while

Have you stopped today and put someone before you

You never know what you might one day need someone to do

Don't Give Up

Hey girl let me talk to you for a minute

Just because you're last in the race doesn't mean you can't win it

Just because there's no silver spoon in your mouth, or diamonds in your ear

Never let anyone stereotype you, or yield to the demon of fear

How do you know what you can do if you never take that chance to begin

Don't depend on anyone else girl, you find the strength from within

Set your goals high and aim straight for the top

Because after you jump that first hurdle, you won't be able to stop

Don't ever let anyone tell you you're not the right color or the right type

We've been held back for too long with all of that crazy hype

See what you must realize is that you don't need anyone to validate you

And once you learn to love yourself, there's no limit to what you can do

Let's take a Stand

All these bombings and shootings are driving me insane

All these murders and kidnappings are weighing heavy on my brain

It seems like the world has gone completely mad

In all of this madness I can't help but feel sad

You got people shooting up airports every other day

We all know this is not the way it's supposed to be

What happened to the days of peace and harmony?

You should never judge someone by the color of their skin

You should take a closer look and see what's within

It's time for us all to rise and take a stand

To show the world that we have a much bigger plan

Let's come together and plot a strategy

To overcome all this hatred and all this tragedy

We should all stand together and be as one

This world has lost too many daughters and too many sons

Somebody please tell when will this insanity end

If we all stand together this battle we can win

It's time for all this mayhem and madness to cease

Who will stand with me for Liberty, Justice, and Peace?

Gifts

Children are gifts sent from Heaven above

Little tiny angels filled with so much love

Their tiny eyes are gleaming, so eager to learn

Not knowing life is full of so many twists and turns

They come into this world alone, alone they shall die

But in between that time they learn from you and I

So we must be very careful of what we say and do

Because your child is learning everything from you

YOU THINK YOU ARE BETTER THAN ME

You think you're better than me, I don't understand

My Bible says that GOD is no respecter of man

You think you're better than me, well I can't really see

Because when GOD made man, he didn't make you any better than me

You think you're better than me, because you go to church every Sunday

Tell me how many times a week do you really get on your knees and pray

You think you're better than me; well it's just not true

And if you really believe that, then GOD BLESS YOU

THEY SAID

They said I wouldn't make it, I wouldn't be here today

But GOD watched over me and sent angels my way

They said I had no future; my life was a big waste

But GOD filled my life with Grace, Mercy, and Faith

They called me worthless, said I was full of sin

But GOD became my roommate, and quickly he moved in

They tried to make me stumble; they tried to make me fall

Not knowing GOD was watching, and one day they'd pay for it all

So you must be very careful of what you say and do

Because the trap you set for me, may very well backfire and trap you

FAITH

Faith is something seen and not heard

Faith is when you don't have to speak a word

Faith is when you smile instead of cry

Faith is when you look the enemy dead in the eye

Faith is when you never give up hop

Faith gives you strength and helps you cope

Faith is also dead without work

Faith keeps you strong even when it hurts

FATHER IN HEAVEN

Father in Heaven I thank you each day

 For loving, forgiving me, and guiding my way

I thank you for loving me, when no one else would

And each time I thought I failed you; you said that I did the best that I could

You are always with me weathering the storm

And when my life was in shambles, you held me in your arms

When my friends and family glared and turned their back

You were always in my corner cutting me some slack

I thought that I carried my corner cutting me some slack

I thought that I carried my weight alone down the road

But you reminded me that you always carried the load

So here I am all polished and brand new and father in Heaven I give all thanks to you

LIFE

Life is up and life is down; sometimes you smile and sometimes you frown

Life has its share of joy and pain; Life is full of sunshine and rain

Life is full of highs and lows; Life is full of hard knock blows

Life is not all fun and games

You always have your share of shame; Life is always pick and choose

Sometimes you win; sometimes you loose

WAITING

I have sat here every day, waiting for this pain to go away

It has not even dulled I have come to realize that it will stay

As a reminder that my life will never be the way it used to be

It's a scar that will forever be visible and will always be with me

There will never be enough time that passes for it to erase

It will haunt me every day and every night there will always be a trace

No matter how fast I run, how many times I smile or how hard I try

This pain is forever etched in me with permanent ink, it's here till I die

Until then I will carry this torch and I will everyday feel the heat from the flame

When you lose someone that you love, you will never ever be the same

TRUE LOVE

IT CANT BE BOUGHT IT CANT BE SOLD

IT'S MORE VALUABLE THAN SILVER AND GOLD

YOU CANNOT GROW IT AND PICK IT FROM A TREE

YOU CAN'T SEE IT WITH YOUR EYES IT'S FOR THE HEART TO SEE

YOU CANNOT MAKE IT OR PUT IT IN A CAN

IT'S THE GIFT THAT GOD BLEW OUT OF HIS HAND

YOU CAN SEARCH FOR IT HIGH AND LOW

YOU CAN TRAVEL ALL OVER THE WORLD TO AND FRO

BUT WHEN THE TIME IS RIGHT AND YOUR HEART IS IN THE RIGHT PLACE

HE WILL REMOVE THE BLINDERS FROM YOUR EYES TO SEE YOUR TRUE LOVES FACE

IF THE LORD IS WILLING

We are so very thankful that God placed you on this earth

And no amount of money could come close to your worth

You worked and you toiled and not once did you complain

You always had a smile even when you were in pain

When God picks flowers he looks for the most beautiful one

Then gently he plucked you because on earth your work was done

You always thought of others always putting your needs aside

You taught us to have faith and in God's word you did abide

We will truly miss you, no one could take your place

You can truly rest now, because you finally won the race

Heaven has a new Angel and earth will never be the same

We pray if the Lord is willing we will see your face again

NEVER BE THE SAME

The moment that you left a part of us went too

The world has never felt so empty now that we don't have you

You have always been here to guide us and show us the way

Now Heaven has an Angel and our blue skies are Grey

Even though we miss you and our hearts are full of pain

We know that you are rejoicing, and one day we will see you again

So as we say goodbye know it is only for a while

Lord willing we will live a life befitting your humble style

When God chooses his flowers he looks for the most beautiful one

Then gently he plucks you because your work on earth is done

Take your rest now there will be no more work to do

You are truly an Angel that's why God selected you.

RUNNING ON E

If someone would have told me that before I was 40, that I would be married and divorced have three children, and have buried one , I would have told them that they were crazy, but this is my story and by the GRACE OF GOD I am still standing.

As I watched them lower my baby into the ground a piece of me went with her. As a parent you never imagine burying your child, for me this was a nightmare and I could not wake up. I was numb as I left the hospital asking myself over and over again did I just leave my baby back there. I remember as if it were yesterday I didn't want anyone in my car or anyone driving me, I put all of my baby's belongings in the front seat and I drove home. I don't remember much of the drive because all I could think of was that I just left my daughter back at the hospital. Tears ran down my face as I drove, thinking of how just yesterday I was picking her up from school because she wasn't feeling well. This can't be happening to me not my baby how could she be gone? I can't explain how I felt when I walked into my house knowing she wasn't going to jump out from somewhere as she always did. My heart was breaking all over again, now I truly knew what the meaning of a broken heart was. I didn't want to speak to anyone as I lay in my bed; I held onto her favorite teddy bear and I cried until I couldn't cry anymore. I heard people in my kitchen laughing. How dare they laugh? My daughter was dead and they were in my kitchen laughing as if they were at a bingo game. I wanted everyone out, how dare they keep living when my world had forever stopped. How dare anyone smile in my house? Carissa Grace was my baby, my heart as I called her my "Minnie me". In an instant my life was forever changed and I wanted everyone and everything to feel my pain. I didn't want to eat; I didn't want to sleep the only thing I wanted was to be able to hold my baby in my arms. Nothing else mattered. I can remember seeing her at the funeral home that whole night all I could think about was leaving her there by herself wanting to go and bring her home. I would hold onto her glasses, anything that smelled like her. I didn't want anyone touching any of her stuff. I wanted things left just the way she left them. It was a process doing all the customary things that needed to be done.

My breaking point was when we had to go make her final arrangements. I was very apprehensive about going into the funeral home. I sat down at the first available seat. Then I slowly turned to the right, and as I read her name on that board it hit me like a ton of bricks that she was dead and she wasn't coming back, that this was real. I remember walking over to the board and running my fingers over her name, and then just sinking to the floor sobbing for my baby. I thought of all the times we shared, of all the things we would never get to do, of all the things that she would never get to do. I would never wish this feeling on anyone. Sitting there as they showed us coffins, and talking about cars, it all was a blur. The one thing I will never forget as long as I live was signing her death certificate, it took every ounce of strength to pick up that pen and sign my name. It just made things so final. I could not leave there quick enough. I can remember us all in the store looking for a dress for her. I'm so used to her running around in the store and wanting everything in sight, and I would have given anything to just hear her voice once more. I believe the entire time I was running on auto pilot, because I can't explain how I made it through those first few days. All I wanted to do was lay down, I felt I would not be able to live without her. At night my chest would hurt so bad that I thought I was having a heart attack. I just knew that soon I would be joining my daughter. Every time I laid my head down or closed my eyes all I could see was her face. I prayed so hard and asked God to keep me from losing my mind. I still had to trust him even though I didn't understand what he was doing. That was the hardest, not questioning God. I was raised in the church and this was definitely the ultimate test of my faith. There were plenty of times when I wanted to break things and smash things, just scream to the top of my lungs but I knew that was not going to bring her back. I sunk into a very deep depression and I did not want to leave my bed. I could not even find the energy to go upstairs, because I knew she wasn't there. I decided I did not want to get up. I laid there and I wallowed in my own self-pity. During the day I would hold it together because I didn't want anyone to see me crying. At night I would cry until I had no more tears. I couldn't hear certain songs, or pass certain store without breaking into tears. Then I started going through all the cards all her classmates sent. My heart was so heavy and yet these children made me smile with all the wonderful things they said about my baby.

So many days I prayed and prayed and prayed, because I didn't know what else to do. I didn't wash, I didn't brush my teeth, and I didn't comb my hair. I didn't care I had given up. Life as I knew it would never be the same, and yet I was still trusting God. I'm not saying it was easy, but my upbringing had taught me to trust God in all situations. My family is no stranger to loosing family members but this was my baby, and it knocked me off my feet. I became angry. I was angry at everyone, especially my boyfriend. He was around me the most and he caught it the most. I have to admit I was angry because no matter what he did it wasn't going to bring my baby back. I didn't want to talk I didn't want company I didn't want to be bothered. The Dr wanted to put me on anti-depressants and I kept saying ok, but I wasn't taking them. I brought her in this world with no medication and it seems I was going to deal with her death the same way. Even though my world has stopped everyone else's was still spinning. It was killing me to see people laughing and smiling and all I could do was cry. Her birthday was so bittersweet as she shared it with her oldest brother. Her school held a memorial and all her family attended with t-shirts adorning her picture. They presented us with photos and school work, and all I could think of is she would have thought this was so cool. We brought cupcakes for her classmates and then we went outside and planted a tree in her memory. I can remember her dad and her brothers digging that hole with such loving care, and as all the helped I just looked around at all the people who were here honoring her on her birthday. We released balloons and watched them disappear into the sky. That day I had to be strong because I realized I still had two sons who were living, and one was celebrating his birthday, and momma needed to make it good for him, and that's what I did. Even though all I wanted to do was crawl in my, bed we had a party for him, and we had two cakes one for him and one for her. I never knew my own strength until now.

I remember reading all of these stories about parents neglecting their children or children getting lost or wondering off, and it took everything in me not to ask God why my child. I can remember driving to work one Sunday morning listening to a sermon on the radio. I and God finally had it out. I had been running around for months telling everyone that I was ok, and that is as fine. Truth is I wasn't fine and this particular I let God know just how I felt. I finally admitted how angry and how hurt I was that he took my baby from me. I really let him know how I felt. I felt better but it didn't bring her back. You know you always feel like no one could ever understand your pain and that you have it the worst. God showed up one afternoon and he showed me. I will never forget this day. I was just going to run to the store, when I back out my drive way I notice the police cars at the house down the street and I knew something wasn't right. A knot formed in the pit of my stomach as I saw someone lying on the grass. I went to the store and was back in five minutes. That's when one of my neighbors told me that someone had committed suicide. I pulled my car into the garage and just started walking that way. I was being led to go. As I walked up everyone looked at me. I remember asking was it a girl and they said yes. The beautiful young lady was 16 years old and my heart sank. I stood there and watched her mother sob for her. Someone said you should go talk to her. I'm thinking what I could possibly say to this woman. As I approached her I just put my arms around her. I began to tell her that she was going to be ok. As I looked to my left there were two young boys who turned out to be her sons. She was saying over and over again I need my baby she was my only girl .At that moment I realized that this woman and myself both had two boys and one girl, and now both our angels were gone.

This was the first time since Carissa died that I actually felt sorry for someone else other than myself. In the middle of my pity Party God showed me that there was someone else out there that was worse than me. It hit me that I was given the luxury of being able to tell my daughter I loved her before she took her last breath, I was there with her. This woman did not get that, and she would forever live with that pain. In an instant I realized that this wasn't just about me anymore and that it was time for sharing with people, to let her know she would be okay. I knew that there was nothing that I could say to make her feel better at that time, so I just stayed and prayed and let her know that one day she would standing in my shoes doing the same thing for someone else. Life is full of ups and downs and we never know where it's going to take us. We just have to keep our faith and keep praying. After that I tried to go back to work and that didn't last, everything made me cry. I just could not focus. I came home and got in my bed, that's where I was most comfortable. I began to question my purpose in life. I began thinking of my son Marcus he always had something positive to say and so many days he encouraged me more than he could ever know. I thought of how he stood by his sister's bed and told her he would live his life for the both of them. My sons kept me sane. In life we never know what will happen but we must surround ourselves with strong faith filled people. It seems when Carissa first died my house was overflowing with people, but that would soon change. It seems after the funeral everyone disappears and you are left to figure it out.

I would go up and down with my mood, I would be crying one minute and fussing the next. I remember going days without sleep and food was not at the top of my priority list either. As a parent you always prepare to leave this earth before your children not the other way around. I know that if it wasn't for God I would have lost my mind, so many nights I would sit up and cry , I would lay in her bed and long to be able to rub her hair while she slept just one more time. Carissa was full of life, she turned everything into something to smile about she always had something funny to say. I would never be able to see that smile again. My pain turned into anger but I would hide it and tell everyone that I was okay, but on the inside I was mad at the world because she wasn't here. I would lash out at the ones closest to me. I would find any reason to be angry to mask the real reason I was mad. It turned me into a cold person and I felt I didn't have any love left to give. It almost felt unfair to love or to be happy. I felt as if I was betraying her to be happy in her absence. I felt guilty if found myself laughing. My world was a complete mess. I couldn't eat or sleep. There is nothing that can prepare you for burying your child. I don't care how many people tell you they know how you feel, it doesn't make the pain go away and it doesn't make you feel any better. Time and prayer is the healer of all wounds. God's grace and mercy kept me through those dark days. He kept me sane and held me in his loving arms. No amount of doctor visits or medication could have brought me through this. I am a true witness that God can restore the most broken person again. I thought I would never be able to be productive again. I thought my life was over. Then I realized that even in my broken mess God had a bigger plan for me. At my darkest hour he was using me to shed light on someone else. When I felt useless, he was using me. When I felt broken he was using me to repair others. When I was ready to give up and quit he allowed others to follow me.

No matter what we are going through God has a purpose even when we can't see it. We have to trust his will and know that He is God. Yes we are broken yes we are hurting, but we have to trust him through the tears, through the pain. Know that in order to enjoy the rainbow, you must endure the rain. Never let anyone put a time table on your healing process. Only you know when you are ready to take the next step. Everyone handles grief differently. There is no rulebook. So don't let anyone judge you because they feel you are moving too fast or too slow. No one knows what you are feeling but you. Take your time and process your feelings. Acknowledge the loss and give yourself time to accept it. I have also found that writing is a great way to deal with grief. It allows you to document your feelings. It also allows you to really be honest with yourself and share things you may not want to share with others. It also allows you to keep up with your progress and also to be able to revisit your feelings. It's also healthy to talk about your loved one. It becomes easier the more you do it. It allows you to keep their memory alive. Especially if you have children. They need to know that it's ok to miss the loved one, and it's ok to talk about them. They need to grieve too. That's what really snapped me out of my funk, because I finally realized I was still needed and that I was still a mother. I had to stop having a pity party and begin to live again for my children that remained here on earth. They still need your love and your attention. It's important to allow children to grieve as well, to talk about the love one and tell you how they feel. My family has suffered so many losses and it seems unreal, but we are still standing by the grace of God. I have buried too many loved ones but burying my daughter was the hardest thing I have ever had to do in my life. I have always been told that God puts no more on you than you can bear; sometimes this load I am carrying seems unbearable. Only to wake up the next day and see I am still here and that He still has His hand on me.

This book is also in loving memory Of Carissa Grace Stover, and every child that has lost their life or lived with childhood asthma.

To God Be The Glory

An excerpt from my new book coming soon.

WHO AM I

My first memories were being in the house with my mom, dad, my brothers and my sister. The best memory I have of my parents together were them standing in our bedroom doorway one Christmas Eve. They were so happy and so were we. We had two cars the perfect little house with a fence and we even had a dog Max. We ran and played and enjoyed our lives. I can remember going to Maryland for the summer and running around with all the kids catching fireflies we didn't have a care in the world. Those were the days that I treasured. Waiting for our grandfather to come home and running to greet him. We all loved that man and he loved us.

I have so many fond memories of being at my great grandmother's house, we ran and played and had so much fun there. We helped her with her garden, we did chores, she didn't take any mess and we loved her. Growing up in my family we had so many people to look after us. They say it takes a village to raise a child and growing up when we did that was exactly the way it was. Everyone could watch you and spank you too. We could run around the neighborhood eat at anyone's house and weren't sacred to walk down the streets, because everyone looked out for each other. Those were the times that I will never forget when life was good, when we had a house two parents, two cars, a dog and a fenced in yard.

I will cherish those times forever, because things changed and they changed quickly. I can remember hearing my parents arguing, and my mom crying. I can remember my dad just not being there one day. Then we would see him every morning as he would walk past our house to catch his ride to work at the stop sign. We were always excited to see him. I can remember a couple of times that he would come to see us and it would always end in him and my mom arguing and we would be sad because his visit would be cut short because it would always end up being about them and not about us.

 Those are the exact words my dad used years later as he described why he wasn't there for us more. He said it became easier not to come because he knew that it would end in an argument about them. After my dad moved out our lives drastically changed. We were what you called latch key kids. My mom was working so we took care of ourselves. Our neighbors would check on us but for the most part we were on our own. Needless to say that we got into more trouble than a little, but we always stuck together. There were always threats but we never told on each other. The day came when we had to move out of the house that we once shared with our dad. Life as we knew it was about to change.

I pray that the words read in this book will inspire or encourage someone.

No matter what comes your way, quitting is not an option.

Tiltles coming soon from Gyfted Ink

It's ok to tell: Melissa Henry Stover

The Thorn in My flesh: Stephanie Dyers

Toby and the freeze cup: Quintin Franklin

A Gyfted Ink Production

TO GOD BE THE GLORY

NOTES

NOTES

FAITH FAVOR GRACE

AUTOGRAPH PAGE

www.ingramcontent.com/pod-product-compliance
Lightning Source LLC
Chambersburg PA
CBHW081158090426
42736CB00017B/3377